Dors

A DOG WALKER'S GUIDE

Nigel Vile

COUNTRYSIDE BOOKS
NEWBURY BERKSHIRE

Countryside Books
3 Catherine Road
Newbury , Berkshire

To view our complete range of books
please visit us at
www.countrysidebooks.co.uk

ISBN 978 1 84674 342 9

Photographs by Nigel Vile

The cover picture shows RG looking out to sea
past Old Harry Rocks

Designed by Peter Davies

Produced by The Letterworks Ltd., Reading
Typeset by KT Designs, St Helens
Printed by The Holywell Press, Oxford

Contents

Walk

Appendix

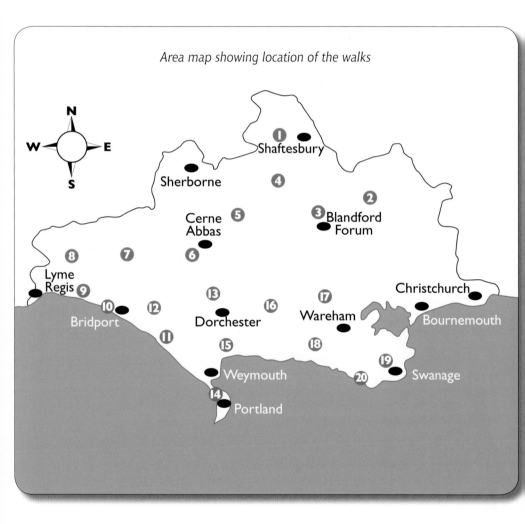

Area map showing location of the walks

INTRODUCTION

I have to confess to having started off as something of a reluctant dog walker – in fact there was even a touch of antipathy towards man's best friend. In a former life, I was always a 'dog free' walker but things changed in 2008 with the birth of my first grandchild. Finn, the family Jack Russell, suddenly found that he was no longer the number one attraction and quite often a walk consisted of little more than a snatched stroll in a nearby park. For a Jack Russell with its love of the great outdoors this must have seemed like purgatory – so in stepped grandfather to fill the occasional void. At first, it was hard work. Finn was little more than a young puppy and, when given the chance to run free, could quite literally disappear. With a little training and the passage of time, however, he has become a lot more sensible and well-behaved, the only exception being when his adopted owner arrives at the house. Such is his excitement, he engages in what can only be described as an outbreak of vertical jumping at the patio doors.

It soon became apparent that choosing a walk for a dog involved special considerations. Roads and traffic, for example were to be avoided if at all possible, as were fields where frisky livestock or sheep and lambs were to be found. Even a slim and agile Jack Russell could find the occasional stile akin to an obstacle course, adding yet another factor to the equation. And then there were the positives to include. Most dogs love chasing sticks, which makes a section of woodland along the way particularly attractive. Woods are also full of exciting scents and sounds, further adding to their appeal. Water is also another attraction, and not only for drinking. Finn enjoys nothing more than diving into a river or pond, in the style of Tom Daley, to retrieve a stick, often providing an amusing sideshow for passing walkers. A pub garden that welcomes dogs is always a must at journey's end, a place to rest and linger awhile at the end of a pleasant few hours in the great outdoors.

This collection of walks in Dorset has been devised with all these factors in mind. Where there are sections of road walking, it is on very quiet country lanes where the chance of meeting vehicles is minimal. If there are stiles, they are those with enough headway and clearance for all but the largest or most immobile dogs to pass through. In such cases, an alternative 'there-and-back' walk has been suggested to ensure a decent walk.

There are walks on heathland near Wareham and Tolpuddle, on open hills at Pilsdon Pen and above Sydling St Nicholas, along the coast at West Bay and Studland ... and so much more in a county with history and intrigue at every turn. The Tolpuddle Martyrs feature here, for example, as does the Cerne Abbas Giant with his total inhibition!

Nigel Vile

ADVICE FOR DOG WALKERS

With open access to the countryside having become something of an issue in recent years, dog owners have to realise that with rights come obvious responsibilities. To quote from an official source 'the countryside is a great place to exercise dogs but it is every owner's duty to make sure their dog is not a danger or nuisance to farm animals, wildlife or other people'. With this in mind, here are a few gentle reminders.

- Some of the coastal walks follow clifftop paths. You know your dog and, if it is at all footloose and fancy free, put it on a lead to avoid a tragic loss of life.

- Ground-nesting birds can often be found on Dorset's downland between March and July. Do not let your dog run free in the area at this time. Equally, pheasants are often released in large numbers into woodland in

the early autumn. Notices requesting that dogs be kept on a lead at this time should obviously be respected.

● Sheep and lambs are by nature nervous creatures. As they turn and run, many dogs find it good fun to give chase. Such behaviour could cause a pregnant ewe to abort so signs warning that dogs worrying sheep could be shot are not there for fun. Lambing time is between January and March.

● Cattle are more often than not simply inquisitive rather than aggressive. A cow who considers her calf to be threatened in some way, however, is a different matter. The stories about walkers being injured by rampaging cows usually involve both calves and dogs. In such cases, the advice is to drop the lead and leave the dog to sort itself out.

● There may well be horses along the way on some of these walks. Horses tend to be very relaxed about both humans and dogs, usually completing ignoring their presence.

● The official source states that it is every dog owner's duty to make sure their dog is not a danger to other people. With this in mind, it goes without saying that any excrement is dealt with properly, and that your dog is not allowed to randomly jump up on other walkers enjoying a few hours in the countryside.

Enough of this necessary 'health and safety' detail, the majority of which is simple common sense and courtesy. With minimal road walking, few stiles, and livestock at a minimum, this is a series of walks that I hope both you and your dog will very much enjoy. I wish you many hours of fun and relaxation walking in Dorset's beautiful countryside

. . . .

PUBLISHER'S NOTE

We hope that you obtain considerable enjoyment from this book; great care has been taken in its preparation. Although at the time of publication all routes followed public rights of way or permitted paths, diversion orders can be made and permissions withdrawn.

We cannot, of course, be held responsible for such diversion orders and any inaccuracies in the text which result from these or any other changes to the routes nor any damage which might result from walkers trespassing on private property. We are anxious though that all details covering the walks are kept up to date and would therefore welcome information from readers which would be relevant to future editions.

The simple sketch maps that accompany the walks in this book are based on notes made by the author whilst checking out the routes on the ground. They are designed to show you how to reach the start, to point out the main features of the overall circuit and they contain a progression of numbers that relate to the paragraphs of the text.

However, for the benefit of a proper map, we do recommend that you purchase the relevant Ordnance Survey sheet covering your walk. The Ordnance Survey maps are widely available, especially through booksellers and local newsagents.

Fontmell Down and Melbury Hill

Melbury Down.

Dorset not only boasts some of the best remaining areas of heathland in Britain, it is also home to some of the best chalk downland, part of which, around Fontmell Down and Melbury Hill, was bought in memory of the English novelist and poet Thomas Hardy, to protect the landscape in which his novels of the Blackmore Vale are set. Here you will discover an open expanse of flowery downland, excellent butterfly populations, and expansive views that stretch for miles across the Blackmore Vale, with superb views of the Saxon town of Shaftesbury to the north. Melbury Beacon, at over 850 ft, was one of the sites used for a warning beacon in centuries past. It was also used as part of a chain of beacons across Dorset to celebrate the Queen's Golden Jubilee. Dogs will enjoy running free on these open hills, but please obey seasonal notices relating to keeping your pet under control when ground-nesting birds are having their young.

Terrain

Most of the walk covers well-defined field paths that cross open downland. However, there is one climb to reach Melbury Beacon.

Where to park

The Fontmell Down car park (GR 886187). **OS map**: Explorer 118 Shaftesbury & Cranborne Chase.

How to get there

Leave the A30 just east of Shaftesbury and follow the B3081 towards Tollard Royal. In just over one mile, where the B3081 turns left, keep ahead on the unclassified road to Melbury Abbas. Having negotiated your way along the narrow winding roads through this village, climb steeply up Spread Eagle Hill to reach the Fontmell Down car park on the right after one mile, ignoring a slightly earlier car park for Melbury Hill. Postcode SP5 5AP.

Nearest refreshments

There are no refreshment facilities on the walk, but there are countless places to enjoy a picnic with views. However, just a few miles away is the Fontmell pub, in the village of Fontmell Magna, where dogs are allowed in the bar area. www.thefontmell.co.uk ☎ 01747 811441. Postcode: SP7 0PA.

Dog factors

Distance: 4½ miles (7.2 km).
Road walking: None.
Livestock: Occasionally sheep will be grazing on some of the downland fields.
Stiles: There is one that could be avoided by doing a simple 'there-and-back' linear walk to Melbury Beacon.
Nearest vets: Longmead Veterinary Practice, Little Content Lane, Shaftesbury, SP7 8PL. www.longmeadvets.co.uk ☎ 01747 852064.

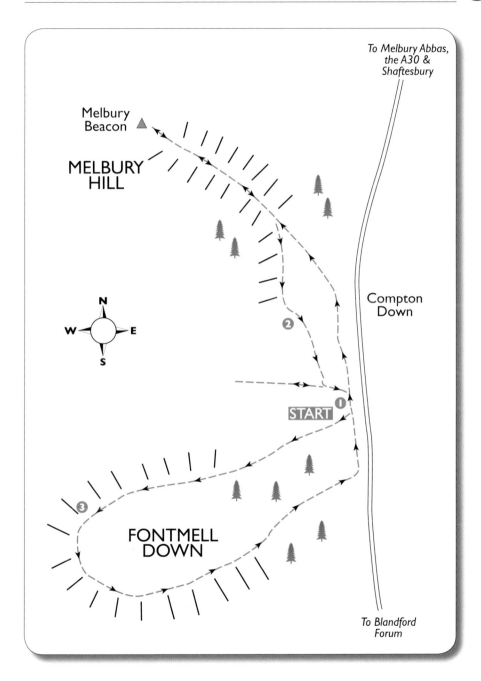

To Melbury Abbas,
the A30 &
Shaftesbury

Melbury
Beacon ▲

MELBURY
HILL

N
W E
S

Compton
Down

START ①

②

③

FONTMELL
DOWN

To Blandford
Forum

The Walk

· ·

1 Walk back up to the road and follow an enclosed footpath on the left that runs parallel to the road in the direction of Shaftesbury. In 250 yards, pass through a handgate at the Melbury Hill parking area and follow the line of a fence ahead, walking towards **Melbury Hill**. Follow the line of this fence for one mile, keeping it on your left, to the top of Melbury Hill. Pass through a handgate on the left to a topograph before following the line of the fence back downhill, again with the fence on the left-hand side. Beyond the 'saddle', follow the fence uphill to a gate in the top corner of the field. Do not pass through this gateway but turn right and follow the line of the fence across **Compton Down**.

2 After 600 yards, bear left where the fence forms a corner. In a few paces, veer right, away from the fence at an angle of about 30 degrees, along a very faint

View to Shaftesbury.

Finn enjoyng the walk.

path to reach a 'hidden' stile in the bottom hedgerow in 200 yards. Cross this stile and drop down some steps to a track. Turn left and follow the track back to the parking area for Fontmell Down. Pass through the gate in the corner of the car park and follow the path ahead on to **Fontmell Down**. In ¾ mile, having passed an area of woodland, go through a gateway on the left bearing a National Trust marker. Veer right in the next field, climbing gently uphill to join the line of a fence which you follow towards the edge of the hilltop.

❸ Follow the fence as it bears left along the western edge of the hilltop. In 100 yards, pass through a gateway on the left and follow the line of a fence across a hilltop field. On the far side of the field, bear right, down to a gate at the bottom right end of a belt of beech trees. Beyond this gate, continue ahead to another gate before walking across the field ahead to reach a dyke. Beyond this earthwork, veer left to a fence and follow it up to the top corner of the field ahead. Pass through a handgate on the left and follow an enclosed path alongside the main road back to the car park.

Pentridge and Cranborne Chase

Finn running free.

Pentridge enjoys a secluded location, lying at the end of a cul de sac lane. Its Celtic name literally translates as 'hill of the boars', a testament to the ancient origins of this settlement. The village features at 'Trantridge' in Thomas Hardy's *Tess of the d'Urbervilles*. The nearby stretch of Cranborne Chase has been described as an 'open-air museum of archaeology' on account of its numerous ancient remains. These include a Bronze Age cursus, an Iron Age hillfort, one of Britain's best stretches of Roman road and Bokerley Ditch, an impressive Romano-British boundary. This was also an historic royal hunting ground where today the 150,000 acres of open chalk grassland, woods and small coppices convey a most regal presence to visitors and their four-footed friends.

Terrain
Well-defined tracks and field paths. There is one climb onto Blagdon Hill.

Where to park
On the grass verge in the vicinity of St Rumbold's church in Pentridge (GR 033179). **OS map**: Explorer 118 Shaftesbury & Cranborne Chase.

How to get there
From the A354, just south of the Hampshire-Dorset border, turn east on a lane signposted to Pentridge. Turn right at a junction in the village, and after a few hundred yards turn right again onto an unmetalled lane to the church and village hall. Postcode SP5 5QX.

Nearest refreshments
There are no refreshment facilities on this walk. The hilltops around Bokerley Ditch, however, offer many excellent picnic spots. The nearest dog-friendly pub is the Roebuck in the village of Sixpenny Handley, three miles from Pentridge (closed Mondays). www.roebuck-inn.com ☎ 01725 552002. Postcode SP5 5NR.

Dog factors
. . . .
Distance: 4 miles (6.4 km).
Road walking: A short section as you leave Pentridge.
Livestock: Occasionally cattle will be found on Blagdon Hill.
Stiles: Four that only the very largest of dogs might struggle with.
Nearest vets: Pilgrims, 5-7 Castle Street, Cranborne, BH21 5PZ.
www.pilgrimsvets.org.uk ☎ 01725 551119.

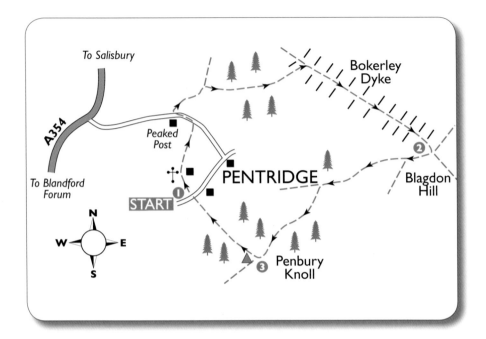

The Walk

. . . .

1 Pass through a gate in the top right corner of the green, to the right of a property. Enter an arable field and turn left. In 250 yards, pass through a gateway and join a lane. Turn left and, on a left-hand bend after 250 yards, turn right along a track, shown on the OS sheet as **Bowling Green Lane**. Keeping right at an early fork, continue for another ½ mile to a crossroads of paths. Keep ahead along an enclosed footpath for 400 yards past an earthwork to reach the **Martin Down National Nature Reserve**. Turn right and follow a path that runs parallel to **Bokerley Dyke**, a linear earthwork.

2 In just over ¾ mile, at a crossroads by a commemorative seat, turn right along a chalk track. In 150 yards, just as the track enters some woodland, follow a bridleway on the right that passes a gateway. 25 yards beyond this gateway, follow a track on the left through another gateway and continue across the hilltop for 600 yards to emerge into an open field. Follow the right edge of this field for 100 yards before bearing left across the open field towards some trees on the far side, a marker post points the direction. Pass through this belt of trees to reach a handgate before walking ahead across the left edge of a hilltop field to reach the wooded summit of **Penbury Knoll**.

3 By a pair of coniferous trees, turn right up to the trig point on the hilltop, (there is no obvious path). At the trig point, turn left and drop downhill for 20 yards before bearing right out of the woodland onto the open hillside. Walk downhill to a stile before continuing to go downhill to another stile in the bottom left corner of the next field. Follow an enclosed path for 350 yards to a stile before crossing a paddock to a stile to the right of gate posts. There is a road after this last stile so dogs should be on a lead here. Turn right along the road before taking the first left, back up to the church and green.

Pentridge church.

Badbury Rings

View to the Rings.

Badbury Rings is an Iron Age hillfort protected by three concentric sets of ramparts and ditches, with the outer rampart being close on one mile in circumference. Legend maintains that this was Mount Badon, where King Arthur defeated the Saxons. An even more far-fetched tale suggests that King Arthur actually lived in the woods on the hilltop disguised as a raven! Whatever the truth in these tales, the views from this chalk knoll are far-ranging and extend from the Purbeck Hills to Cranborne Chase. Beyond this ancient earthwork lie mile after mile of ancient drove tracks that cross an open expanse of the Dorset countryside. Some of these were former Roman roads that formed a complex junction on the north side of the rings. These roads ran to such places as the hillfort on Hod Hill, Dorchester and to Old Sarum. Whatever the intricacies of this network of tracks, dogs will simply enjoy running free, unencumbered by either livestock or traffic.

Dog factors

Distance: 4 miles (6.4 km).
Road walking: None.
Livestock: None.
Stiles: None.
Nearest vets: Friars Moor Vets, Higher Shaftesbury Road, Blandford Forum, DT11 8ST. www.friarsmoorvets.co.uk ☎ 01258 472160.

Terrain
Well-defined tracks that cross a flat and easy-to-walk landscape.

Where to park
In the National Trust car park at Badbury Rings (GR 961032). **OS map**: Explorer 118 Shaftesbury & Cranborne Chase.

How to get there
Badbury Rings lies alongside the B3082, midway between Blandford Forum and Wimborne Minster. This ancient monument is clearly signposted. Postcode DT11 9GL.

Nearest refreshments
There are no refreshment facilities on the walk, but Badbury Rings and its environs would be an excellent spot for a picnic. The nearest pub is the Anchor Inn at Shapwick, which is down a lane opposite the entrance to the Badbury Rings site. The Anchor even provides dog biscuits if you happen to have forgotten your own! www.anchorshapwick.co.uk ☎ 01258 857269. Postcode DT11 9LB.

Dorset – A Dog Walker's Guide

The Walk

. . . .

1 Pass through a handgate in the top left corner of the car park, with Badbury Rings away on the right, and follow the path ahead to a gate. Continue along a gravelled path that passes through some woodland before reaching a junction, just under ½ mile from the car park. Turn left and, in a few paces, right, to follow the **Hardy Way**. After ¼ mile turn left at a junction and follow a track for 600 yards to another junction.

2 Turn right onto a gated bridleway and follow the track ahead for ¾ mile, past **Lambing Cottage**, to a point where a track comes in on the left. Continue ahead for another 50 yards before passing through a gap in the hedgerow on the right to follow a bridleway across an arable field. Pass a pair of tumuli in 350 yards, and continue across to a gate in the left-hand hedgerow, and a track. Turn right and follow this track for 400 yards to a crossroads.

3 Turn right and follow the **King Down Drove** for ¾ mile to a crossroads a little way beyond a property called Highwood Cottage. Turn left on the path signposted to Badbury Rings and continue for 400 yards to a junction by a

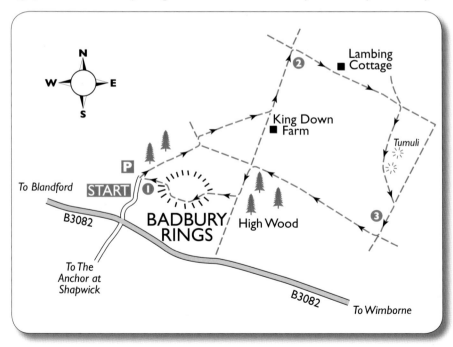

Flax fields.

small copse. Pass through a gateway on the right to enter the Badbury Rings National Trust property. Walk across to the rings and follow the earthworks to the left for ¼ mile to the far side of the ramparts. Turn left along a gravelled path that leads back to the car park.

Hod Hill

Woodland path by the Stour.

Hod Hill is the site of Dorset's largest Iron Age settlement, a site of some 54 acres that protected the important Stour valley. The fort sits proudly atop a glorious chalk hilltop, awash with flora in summer months, with commanding views across the Stour. The site was not impregnable, however, falling to the Second Augustan Legion during the first few years of the Roman conquest. The Romans constructed a fort of their own in the north-west corner of the site, where as many as 700 men and 250 horses were garrisoned. To escape the heavy hand of history, this walk also includes a delightful woodland path along the banks of the river Stour back to Stourpaine, where Holy Trinity church sits at the southern end of the main street facing a large number of attractive brick and flint cottages. Dogs will love this walk, with its traffic-free tracks and field paths where they can run free.

Terrain
Well-defined tracks and field paths with one steep climb onto Hod Hill. The path alongside the river Stour can be muddy following heavy rain

Where to park
On the roadside by Holy Trinity church in Stourpaine (GR 860094). OS map: Explorer 118 Shaftesbury & Cranborne Chase.

How to get there
Stourpaine lies 3 miles north of Blandford Forum on the A350 Shaftesbury road. Turn into South Holme, alongside the White Horse Inn, and then left at its junction with Manor Road. Holy Trinity church lies at the end of Manor Road. Postcode DT11 8JZ.

Nearest refreshments
The White Horse Inn at Stourpaine welcomes dogs in the bar, on the decking area and seated out at the front. Food is served every day from 12 noon until 9 pm, with the exception of Mondays when the kitchen closes at 5.30 pm. When dining at the White Horse, you will be in good company. HRH Prince Charles and the Duchess of Cornwall paid a visit in May 2011. www.whitehorse-stourpaine.co.uk ☎ 01258 453535. Postcode: DT11 8TA.

Dog factors
· ·
Distance: 3 miles (4.8 km).
Road walking: Short sections of road walking in Stourpaine where dogs are best kept on leads.
Livestock: Occasionally sheep will be found grazing on Hod Hill.
Stiles: None.
Nearest vets: Damory Veterinary Clinic, Edward Street, Blandford Forum, DT11 7QT. www.damoryvets.co.uk ☎ 01258 452626.

The Stour.

The Walk

. . . .

1 With your dog on a lead as you pass through the village, walk back along **Manor Road**, beyond its junction with South Holme and continue for 250 yards to a point where the road bears right up to the A350. Keep ahead on a side lane, passing **Stour Vale Cottage** on the right. Continue along the lane until it ends by property number 43 and continue on a path that borders the river Irwerne. Follow this path to a junction in 200 yards, before keeping left on the public bridleway.

2 After ¼ mile, enter the National Trust's **Hod Hill** property and walk ahead for 30 yards to reach the second rampart of the hillfort. Climb the rampart on

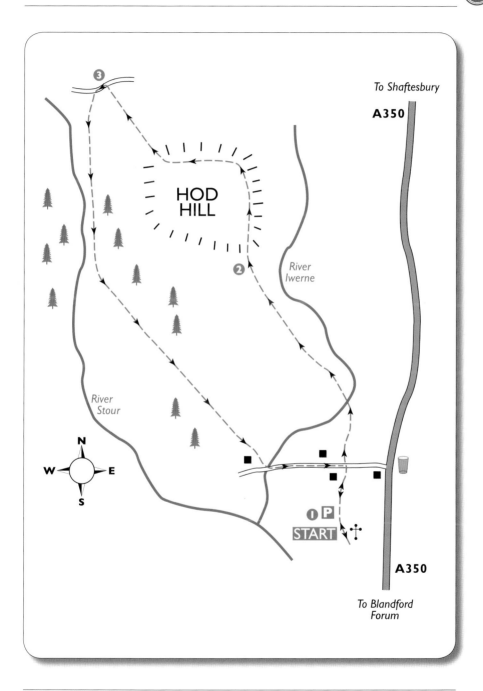

the right and follow its course around the eastern and northern sides of the hilltop to reach the north-west corner of the hillfort. At this point, follow a track to the right down to a handgate below the ramparts. Beyond this gate, walk down the left edge of the hillside field ahead to a gate in its bottom left corner. Drop downhill for 25 yards to a parking area over on the right.

3 At this point, take the second of two left turns and follow a bridleway that shortly borders the **River Stour** on the right. Follow the Stour for 600 yards before keeping on the track as it bears left away from the river. This is shown on the OS map as **Hod Drive**. In ½ mile, at a junction by Iwerne Cottage, and with your dog now back on a lead, turn left into the centre of Stourpaine and return to **Manor Road**. Turn right, back to Holy Trinity church.

Milton Abbas

Milton Abbas.

So many villages claim the adjective 'picture-postcard' but Milton Abbas can genuinely lay claim to this title. The village holds the distinction of being the first planned settlement in England. It was founded in 1780 when Lord Milton, Earl of Dorchester, decided that the old village ruined the view from his new mansion at nearby Milton Abbey. So he set about moving the entire village over the hill! Sir William Chambers was the architect responsible for carrying out the earl's wishes, and he created a delightful community of whitewashed and thatched cottages lining a broad street. Our four-legged friends will no doubt have little interest in this historic detail, preferring instead to get out to the vast areas of mixed woodland to the east of the village made up of Milton Park and Charity Woods, Oatclose and Cliff Woods. Particular highlights will be the bluebells and other spring flora, as well as butterfly species that include the silver-washed fritillary.

Terrain
Well-defined tracks and paths but do follow the instructions carefully – or risk getting lost in deep woodland! A compass might prove useful on this walk.

Where to park
On the roadside at the Hambro Arms in Milton Abbas (GR 808019). **OS map**: Explorer 117 Cerne Abbas & Bere Regis.

How to get there
Leave the A354 at Winterborne Whitechurch, five miles south-west of Blandford Forum, and follow an unclassified road signposted to Milton Abbas. The Hambro Arms is at the top end of the main street in the village. Postcode DT11 0BP.

Nearest refreshments
There are picnic tables outside the Hambro Arms where dogs and their owners can enjoy rest and refreshment at the end of the walk. Food is served at lunchtimes and in the evenings, apart from on Mondays when the pub is closed. www.hambroarms.com ☎ 01258 880233. Postcode DT11 0BP.

Dog factors
Distance: 6 miles (9.6 km).
Road walking: Small sections in Milton Abbas.
Livestock: None.
Stiles: None.
Nearest vets: Damory Veterinary Clinic, Damory Lodge, Edward Street, Blandford Forum, DT11 7QT. www.damoryvets.co.uk
☎ 01258 452626.

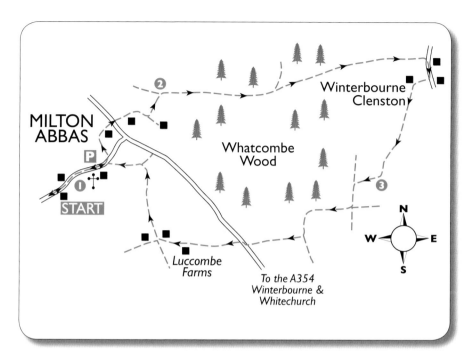

The Walk

. . . .

1 With your back to the Hambro Arms, follow the road to the right, uphill and out of Milton Abbas. In 150 yards, a few paces past a picnic site, follow a footpath on the left, signposted to Haydon Plantation. Follow this path up to a road and continue around to a junction with **Catherine's Well**. Follow this road to the right to a crossroads before joining the lane opposite that gives access to a number of properties. In 250 yards, beyond the entrance to Milton Manor, continue along an unmetalled road that heads into **Milton Park Wood**. After 250 yards, where the track bears right into a private property, follow the signposted bridleway on the left for 300 yards to a junction with another track. Turn left and, in a few paces, right, then continue on the bridleway for 50 yards to another junction.

2 Turn right and follow a track through the woodland for ¾ mile to a crossroads. Continue ahead for 40 yards, climbing uphill to a fork. Take the right-hand bridleway and continue for 200 yards to a barrier at the edge of the woodland. Beyond this barrier, follow a bridleway along the left edge of a field for ¾ mile to a road on the edge of **Winterborne Clenston**. You may want to put your dog on a lead here. Turn right and, in 300 yards, turn right again onto a track opposite a thatched barn and just past the Old Rectory. Follow this track for 250 yards up to Clenston Lodge on the right. Just past this property, where the track bears right and is signposted as 'Private', keep ahead along a bridleway that enters **Oatclose Wood**. In 600 yards, at a junction, keep ahead, ignoring the path going off to the right. Ignoring all side turns, follow the path ahead for 450 yards to a gate on the edge of the woodland and an open field.

3 Pass to the right of the gate, turn right and drop downhill to a junction with a path in the bottom of a valley. Turn left and, in 350 yards, at a crossroads, turn right. In 400 yards, at a fork, take the bridlepath that goes off on the left. Keep on this path as it climbs uphill into an open field, follow the left edge of this field to its corner before turning right to follow the end field boundary for ¼ mile. Dogs on leads here as you are approaching a road. Cross the road and follow the driveway opposite, down to **East Luccombe Farm** with its various businesses. Beyond the farm, continue for 250 yards up to Dairy Cottages. Immediately past these cottages, turn right and follow a track for 300 yards along to an arable field. Follow the right edge of this field and, almost in its far corner, follow a path on the left signposted to Milton Abbas. Walk across to a

gate by a telegraph pole at the entrance to some woodland. Follow the path downhill through the woodland to the road in the village before turning left back to the Hambro Arms.

A quiet woodland path.

The Cerne Abbas Giant

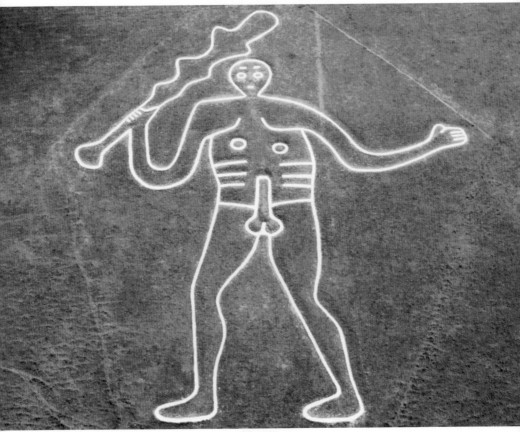

The Giant.

Cerne Abbas, nestling deep in the Cerne valley, is a beautiful stone, brick and flint village that must surely rank as one of the most handsome settlements in all Dorset. A Benedictine abbey was founded here in the 10th century, the remains of which can still be seen in a field by St Mary's church. The church itself is worth visiting to see its 15th-century rood screen, a Jacobean pulpit with its canopy or 'tester' and 14th-century wall paintings in the chancel. To the north of Cerne Abbas rises Giant Hill, on whose slopes is carved a massive 180 ft hill figure – who is not afraid to display his modesty! Beyond the Giant lies an ancient earthwork known as the 'Trendle' that was the site of ancient May Day rituals until recent times. This is an intriguing walk with views across the mysterious Wessex landscape, and fields awash with flora in the spring and summer months. It is a perfect dog walk with few 'hindrances' along the way and a cool stream at journey's end for those water-loving pooches.

Dog factors

Distance: 3 miles (4.8 km).
Road walking: : There are short sections of road walking in Cerne Abbas where dogs should be on a lead.
Livestock: Occasionally sheep will be found grazing on Giant Hill.
Stiles: None.
Nearest vets: Castle Veterinary Clinic, Poundbury Business Centre, Poundbury, Dorchester DT1 3WA. www.castlevets.co.uk ☎ 01305 267083

Terrain
Well-defined tracks and field paths with one steep climb onto Giant Hill.

Where to park
Long Street, the main road in Cerne Abbas, in the vicinity of the New Inn (GR 665012). **OS map**: Explorer 117 Cerne Abbas & Bere Regis.

How to get there
Cerne Abbas lies eight miles north of Dorchester on the A352 Sherborne Road. Leave the main road and drive into the centre of the village, parking on Long Street as close to the New Inn as possible. Postcode DT2 7JF.

Nearest refreshments
The Royal Oak on Long Street in Cerne Abbas is a dog-friendly pub with plenty of outdoor seating for hot sunny days. The pub is open from 11 am to 3 pm and from 6 pm until 11 pm every day, and serves sandwiches and snacks as well as hearty meals. ☎ 01300 341797. Postcode DT2 7JG.

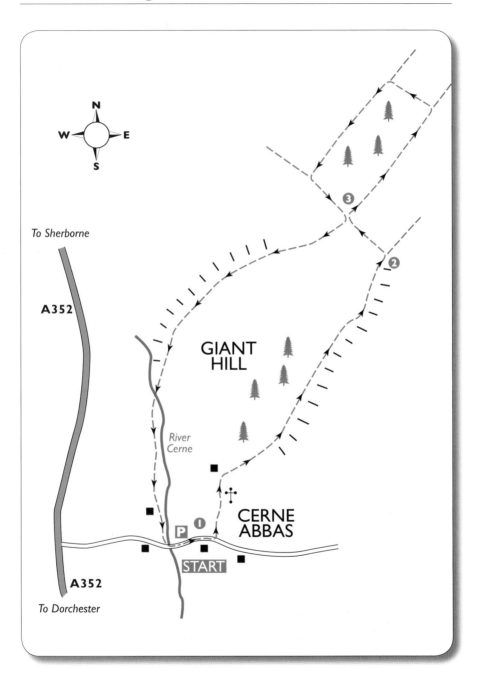

The Walk

1 With your dog on a lead and your back to the New Inn, follow Long Street to the right, along to the Royal Oak. Turn left into **Abbey Street** and walk up past the church towards Cerne Abbey. Turn right just before the abbey into a churchyard and, at an immediate junction, bear left on a path signposted to the Giant Hill. Pass through a gate on the far side of the churchyard before turning right to some woodland on the edge of **Giant Hill**. Continue to a handgate before following a path that borders the wooded slopes of the hillside to reach a stile and a bridleway. Follow this bridleway to the left, climbing steadily to reach the hilltop.

2 Beyond a gate, walk across the left edge of a hillside field to the next gate. Follow a short section of track to a gate on the left, before crossing an open field and reaching a small copse. Turn right just before this copse and follow the bottom left edge of a field for 250 yards to a path on the left, signposted

River Cerne.

to Minterne Parva. Follow this path across a field to a gate and junction before turning left along a path signposted to Cerne Abbas. In ¼ mile, just past a handgate, turn left up to another handgate and the small copse passed earlier.

3 Just past this copse, at a crossroads of paths, turn right and follow a footpath across the hilltop to a stile. Continue following the well-worn path across and then down the hillside to the bottom of the enclosure containing the Cerne Abbas Giant. Drop down some steps to a junction and follow a path on the right signposted to Kettle Bridge. Follow this path down to a barn, turn left and at the next junction, turn right down to Kettle Bridge. Cross the bridge and follow a path to the left that borders the **River Cerne**. Ignoring side turns, continue for 250 yards to Mill Cottage. With your dog back on a lead, keep ahead on Mill lane to **Duck Street** before continuing to **Long Street** and the New Inn.

Sydling St Nicholas

A green lane.

Sydling St Nicholas enjoys a remote and off-the-beaten-track location, surrounded on all sides by some of Dorset's finest downland. The diminutive Sydling Water flows through the village, where Pevsner wrote at length about the church, the adjoining Court House and the tithe barn. The village was recorded in the Domesday Book, although evidence of much earlier human occupation has been found in the surrounding area. The OS map, for example, shows countless tumuli, settlements and barrows on the nearby hills. It is these hills that form the focus of this walk, many of them being open access land that has escaped the ravages of the plough and pesticides. The result is unimproved chalk grassland, home to a rich array of flora and fauna in season. Amongst the various species are vetch, scabious, milkwort and betony, which in turn attract butterfly species that can include the rare adonis blue as well as the marsh fritillary. All of this natural history will be lost on dogs, who will enjoy running free on the open downland, subject to the usual advice about using a lead if there are sheep grazing on the hilltops.

Terrain
Well-defined field paths and tracks; one climb onto the downs at the beginning.

Where to park
At the southern end of Sydling St Nicholas, by a small green dominated by a huge chestnut tree, turn into Church Lane where there is room for roadside parking (GR 632994). **OS map**: Explorer 117 Cerne Abbas and Bere Regis.

How to get there
Leave the A352 at Cerne Abbas and follow an unclassified road west, signposted to Sydling. In two miles, by a ford, turn left and drive into Sydling St Nicholas, making for a small green at the southern end of the village opposite the village hall. Postcode DT2 9PA.

Nearest refreshments
The Greyhound Inn in Sydling St Nicholas is a dog-friendly pub. Serving 'proper' food that changes every day, and with various good food awards, the Greyhound is open from 11 am to 3 pm and 5.30 pm to 11 pm, and all day on Sundays. www.dorsetgreyhound.co.uk ☎ 01300 341303. Postcode DT2 9PD.

Dog factors
Distance: 5½ miles (8.8 km).
Road walking: A small section in Sydling St Nicholas.
Livestock: One or two fields along the way might contain sheep, so be aware.
Stiles: None.
Nearest vets: Girling and Bowditch Veterinary Surgeons, Bull Lane, Maiden Newton, DT2 0BQ. www.beaminstervets.co.uk.
☎ 01308 862312.

The Walk

1 Walk back down to the High Street and follow **East Street** opposite, past the village hall. In 150 yards, with a property on the left called 'Hit and Miss', take the right turn signposted to Hog Hill that runs along the end of a recreation ground. At the end of the recreation ground, and by the last property on the left, continue along a driveway for 25 yards before taking the left turn, again signposted to Hog Hill. In 350 yards, where the farm track bears right, pass through a gateway into a field ahead and follow the Wessex **Ridgeway** ahead across two fields. Walk across the following field, bearing left all the while, to a visible gate in a fence at the top of the field. Do not

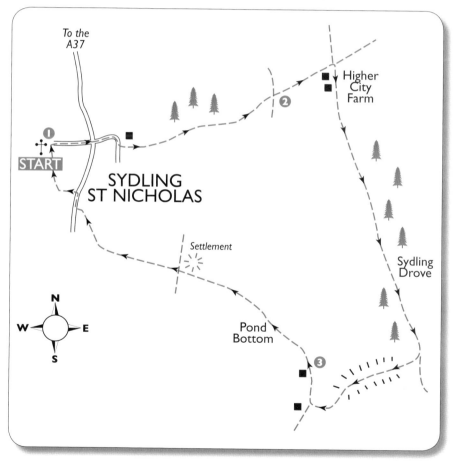

pass through this gateway but follow the line of the fence to the left for 250 yards to a point where the fence forms a corner.

2 Pass through a gate on the right at this point and follow the left edge of a field to a gap in the hedge opposite. Continue along a farm track to a copse before crossing the hilltop to **Higher City Farm**. By the farm, turn right to pass a barn and bungalow before following a track across open countryside to a gate. Cross a field, pass through another gate and continue following what is signposted as Sydling Drove across open access land. Pass through a gate at the end of the field and follow the bridleway across the right edge of the next field. Beyond the next gate, with a memorial stone on the left, cross a field to a gate opposite and enter one final field with a natural bowl in the hillside on the right. Bear right over to this bowl, pass through a gate and follow a path downhill signposted to Crete Bottom. In ¼ mile, at a junction at the bottom of the hill, turn right and follow a bridleway through a delightful valley.

In Crete Bottom.

③ Beyond a gate, continue walking through the valley, shortly passing a tin barn on the right. In 400 yards, where the fence on the left forms a corner, keep on the track as it bears left to climb gently uphill. Beyond a gate, continue along an enclosed track for 350 yards to a junction. The bumps in the ground on the right are shown on the OS map as '**Settlement**'. Follow the concrete farm road opposite downhill for ¼ mile before bearing right by a barn and walking along to **Huish Farm**. You will be passing through a farm and crossing a road shortly so dogs should be on a lead now. Follow the right of way to the left through the farm complex to reach the road leading into Sydling St Nicholas. Turn right and, in 25 yards, left, onto a bridleway. After 175 yards, at a junction, turn right and follow a track for 200 yards to a barn on the left. Continue for 50 yards to a tithe barn on the left, turning left immediately before this barn. Just past the tithe barn, enter the village churchyard by way of a dog-friendly stile. Walk through the churchyard and, once past the church, follow a driveway on the right, back down to Church Lane.

Pilsdon Pen

Barrow on Pilsdon Pen.

The West Dorset countryside, remote and accessible by what are generally narrow and winding lanes, has never been as popular with walkers as the coast or the better-known eastern part of the county. This makes for a rather unspoilt landscape that is truly far from Hardy's proverbial madding crowd. Pilsdon Pen, at 909 ft, is the second highest point in Dorset, only overshadowed by nearby Lewesdon Hill. Both hills stand guard on the northern slopes of the lush Marshwood Vale, and look in a southerly direction towards Lyme Bay. Sitting proudly on top of Pilsdon Pen is an Iron Age hillfort, replete with two Bronze Age burial mounds, evidence that this lonely hilltop was occupied long before the hillfort was built. The site has also revealed flint tools dating back over 10,000 years. The views are far-ranging and encompass an area where dogs will enjoy running free, subject to the usual provisos about using leads in the presence of livestock.

Terrain

Field paths and tracks that cross an undulating landscape; some ascents around Pilsdon Pen.

Where to park

The Pilsdon Pen car park (GR 414009). **OS map**: Explorer 116 Lyme Regis & Bridport.

How to get there

Turn off the A3066 at Beaminster and follow the B3163 to Broadwindsor. In the village, take the B3164 signposted to Lyme Regis. In 2 miles, park in a lay-by at the foot of Pilsdon Pen, which is on the right-hand side of the road. Postcode DT6 5NZ.

Nearest refreshments

Pilsdon Pen is an ideal spot for a picnic. The nearest dog-friendly pub is the White Lion in Broadwindsor, which is open lunchtimes and evenings, apart from Monday lunchtime. This is a Palmers pub that serves fine local ales. ☎ 01308 867070. Postcode DT8 3QD.

Dog factors
. . . .

Distance: 3 miles (4.8 km).
Road walking: None.
Livestock: Occasionally on the hilltops.
Stiles: There is one that will prove difficult for large dogs.
Nearest vets: Girling and Bowditch Veterinary Surgeons, Beaminster, DT8 3HB. www.beaminstervets.co.uk ☎ 01308 862312.

The Walk
. . . .

❶ Cross the road, pass through the gateway opposite and walk steeply uphill on what is the National Trust's **Pilsdon Pen**. In 50 yards, where the path bears

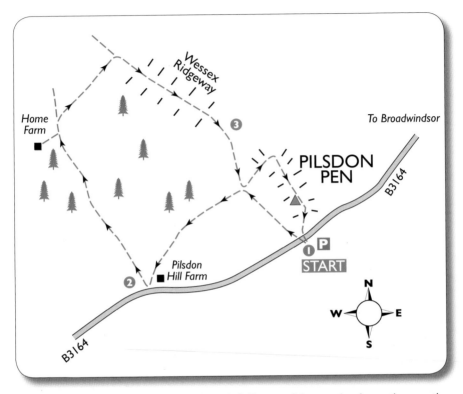

right to some steps, keep ahead and follow a faint path along the south-western flank of Pilsdon Pen. Walk along to the far left-hand corner of the NT property and, beyond a line of beech trees, pass through a gateway. Put your dog on a lead before following a track downhill to the left to a road by **Pilsdon Hill Farm**. Turn right and, in a few paces, right again into a field following a bridleway.

2 Follow this bridleway across the left edges of three fields to reach a track by a barn. Head along this track to a fork in 300 yards and veer right onto a grassy path, ignoring an earlier left turn shown on the OS map as **Attisham Lane**. In 200 yards, pass through a gateway on the right to follow a path uphill signposted to Speckett Cottage. At the top of the climb, pass through a handgate and turn right to walk along the top right edge of a hilltop field. At the end of the field, pass through a gateway and cross the next field on a permissive link to the **Wessex Ridgeway**. Pass through the left-hand of two gateways ahead, and follow the right edge of a field to a gate and stile in its corner.

3 Cross the large field ahead, bearing right all the while, to a gate in the right-hand field boundary almost in the far corner of the field. Continue down a track to a gate by the line of beech trees passed earlier in the walk. Turn left and pass through another gate, turn left and follow the line of a fence uphill onto **Pilsdon Pen**. On the hilltop, having passed the upper rampart, turn right and follow the rampart along to the trig point. Pass to the left of the trig point, drop down through the ramparts to a seat before following a stepped path downhill to a gate and the parking area.

Beech avenue.

Stonebarrow Hill

Trig point – Golden Cap.

This spectacular walk east of Charmouth explores a landscape of rolling hills and pastoral fields, sunken lanes and ancient hedgerows, as well as some of the most dramatic coastline in Dorset. From the wide open expanses of Stonebarrow Hill, our steps drop downhill into the diminutive hamlet of Stanton St Gabriel where a ruinous chapel hides a sad if romantic story. Two newly-weds were cast ashore here in a storm and prayed to St Gabriel for their salvation. When they were saved, the husband promised to build a chapel on the site, only for his wife to die in his arms. Towering above

St Gabriel's is Golden Cap, at 626 ft the highpoint on Britain's southern coast. The name comes from the colouration of the cliff's summit, where sandstone and gorse reflect a golden hue in bright sunlight. Beyond Golden Cap lies an area of undercliff where the sea has eroded a very fragile coastline. Bush and scrub have now colonised the rock falls, caused by the slippage of harder rock strata that sat upon softer clay giving rise to an irregular landscape of peaks, gullies and slipped blocks. With steep cliffs, ensure that lively dogs are kept on leads in places.

Dog factors

Distance: 5 miles (8 km).
Road walking: None.
Livestock: None. **Stiles:** None.
Nearest vets: Bredy Veterinary Centre, Sea Road North, Bridport, DT6 4RR. www.bredyvets.co.uk ☎ 01308 456771.

Terrain
Well-defined tracks and paths; a couple of steep ascents, especially if you detour to the summit of Golden Cap.

Where to park
The National Trust's Stonebarrow Hill car park (GR 383933). **OS map**: Explorer 116 Lyme Regis & Bridport.

How to get there
At the eastern end of the main road in Charmouth, where it bears left towards the A35, turn right onto Stonebarrow Lane. After 1 mile, at the top of a climb, the road becomes unmetalled. Follow this road for ¾ mile, passing two car parks and a National Trust shop, before the unmetalled road ends at a final car park. Postcode DT6 6RA.

Nearest refreshments
There are no refreshment facilities on this walk, but there are plenty of excellent picnic possibilities with fine coastal views. Back in Charmouth, the Royal Oak welcomes dogs on leads. Open all day and every day, with simple good-quality food served between 12 noon and 2.30 pm and 5.30 pm to 8.30 pm, the pub serves Palmers ales from nearby Bridport. www.royaloakcharmouth. com ☎ 01297 560277. Postcode DT6 6PE.

The Walk

. . . .

1 Pass through a gateway in the back corner of the parking area signposted to **Chardown Hill** and Morcombelake. Follow a track for ½ mile to a gate and a drive on the left to Grand View Farm. Follow the quiet lane ahead for 300 yards downhill before turning right onto a track to Golden Cap. In ¾ mile, at Pickaxe Cross, follow the track opposite towards St Gabriel's and Golden Cap.

2 Follow the track for 600 yards through to **St Gabriel's Cottages**, turn left, signposted to Golden Cap, and walk up to the remains of St Gabriel's church. Pass through a gateway beyond the church and follow the path to the right up to a junction below Golden Cap. If you are feeling energetic, detour to the left up to the summit of **Golden Cap**, the highest point on the south coast. For the main walk, follow the Coast Path to the right, signposted to Charmouth.

St Gabriel's.

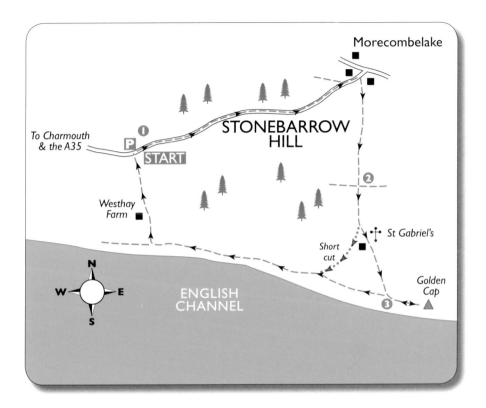

NOTE: to avoid a steep climb on the lower slopes of Golden Cap, bear right on reaching St Gabriel's Cottages to a gate just below a stone outbuilding and a wooden shed. Beyond this gate, follow a path through to the Coast Path and turn right towards Charmouth.

❸ The **Coast Path** is clearly signed so directions are unnecessary. Simply follow the path for 1¾ miles to a right turn signposted to Chardown Hill using the **Smugglers' Path**. Follow this path ahead, ignoring any side turns, for ¾ mile back to the parking area.

West Bay and Burton Bradstock

Path to East Cliff.

If **many of the locations in this walk seem** strangely familiar, it is because this was the corner of Dorset that featured in the ITV crime thriller *Broadchurch*. The iconic East Cliff featured in so many scenes, and it was on the beach below these sandstone cliffs that the body of young Danny

Latimer was found. Further east, one of the caravans in the Freshwater Beach Holiday Park was where that feisty character Susan Wright – played by Pauline Quirke – made her home. And West Bay's picturesque harbour, originally a commercial port that exported so many of the ropes and nets made in nearby Bridport, was a prime location in many of the scenes. This splendid coastal walk, with the sights and sounds of the sea, will prove an absolute delight for dogs, but do use leads on the top of East Cliff if your pooch's behaviour is at all unpredictable – it is a long drop down to the beach!

Dog factors

Distance: 4½ miles (7.2 km).
Road walking: A short section of quiet lane in Burton Bradstock; keep your dogs under control in the Freshwater Beach Holiday Park.
Livestock: None.
Stiles: None.
Nearest vets: Bredy Veterinary Centre, Sea Road North, Bridport, DT6 4RR. www.bredyvets.co.uk ☎ 01308 456771.

Terrain
Well-defined coastal paths.

Where to park
The East Beach car park in West Bay (GR 464903). **OS map**: Explorer 117 Cerne Abbas and Bere Regis.

How to get there
Follow the B3157 into West Bay from Bridport. On reaching a junction in this fishing port, turn left towards the West Bay Hotel and use a car park on the right, almost opposite the hotel. Postcode DT6 4EW.

Nearest refreshments
The bar area of the West Bay Hotel is dog-friendly. The opening times depend upon the season but are essentially lunchtimes and evenings in the winter and 12 noon until 11 pm in the summer season. www.thewestbayhotel.co.uk ☎ 01308 422157. Postcode DT6 4EW. There is also the dog-friendly Hive Beach Café at the halfway point that serves excellent locally-caught seafood and fish. www.hivebeachcafe.co.uk ☎ 01308 897070. Postcode DT6 4RF.

The Walk

. . . .

1 Walk across the shingle beach by the car park, turn left and climb uphill onto **East Cliff**. Follow the **Coast Path** for one mile until it drops downhill into a caravan park at **Freshwater Beach**. Keep your dog on a lead as you pass through the caravan park. Continue following the Coast Path ahead, sand and shingle on the right, until the path reaches the **river Bride**. Turn left and follow a grassy path through a campsite to a gate on the right and a bridge over the river Bride in 300 yards.

2 Cross the bridge and turn left, signposted to Burton Bradstock. In 250 yards, beyond a gate, follow a quiet back lane into **Burton Bradstock**. You may want to put your dog on a lead here. In 150 yards, at a junction, cross to a path opposite to the right signposted to Burton Beach. Follow this stepped path up to a stile and follow the path ahead along the left edge of a field before walking diagonally across the field to a gate and marker post (detour left to Hive Beach Café on Burton Beach). Turn right and walk across to the far side of the field on the Coast Path.

3 Cross a lane and pass through a gateway opposite to enter the National Trust Burton Bradstock property. Follow the Coast Path for just over ½ mile to a

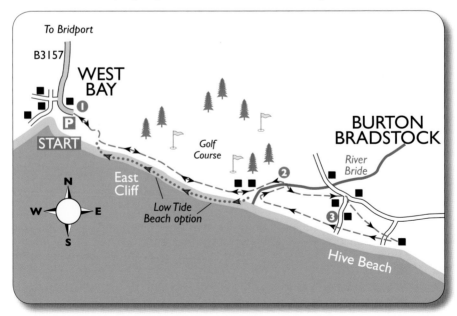

handgate on the right and a signpost pointing the way to West Bay. Turn right and follow the river Bride inland for 250 yards to a footbridge on the left. Cross this bridge, turn left and continue following the Coast Path through a campsite, with your dog on a lead, towards West Bay. In 600 yards, just past the last caravan, follow a path uphill onto **East Cliff** and retrace your steps along the Coast Path for one mile back into West Bay. *NOTE: If the tide is receding, rather than retracing your steps over East Cliff back to West Bay, you could follow the beach below the cliffs.*

On the beach.

Abbotsbury and Chesil Beach

Chesil Beach.

Abbotsbury was described as 'very pleasantly situated among the downs' by Sir Frederick Treves (author of *Highways and Byways in Dorset*, 1906), whilst Ralph Wightman (1950s broadcaster and author) was of the opinion that the village was 'possibly the most interesting in Dorset'. The interest is generated by a swannery, sub-tropical gardens and some surviving abbey buildings that include St Catherine's chapel, a 14th-century pilgrimage chapel that stands on a hill between the village and the nearby coast. The swannery, incidentally, is the world's only managed colony of nesting mute swans. On the downland above the village stands Abbotsbury Castle, an Iron Age hillfort that in its day was the frontline of defence from invasion on account of its commanding outlook across the England Channel. The view from the fort takes in Chesil Beach, described locally as 'the eighth wonder of the world', whose 18 miles of pebbles stretch from Portland to Burton Bradstock. The section between Portland and Abbotsbury encloses a vast brackish lagoon known as The Fleet that was immortalised in John Meade Faulkner's novel *Moonfleet*. All of this detail will be lost on dogs, who will simply enjoy running free on the downland hilltops or on the margins of Chesil Beach.

Terrain
Well-defined tracks and field paths. The pebbles of Chesil Beach are avoided by using a very quiet access road that runs to its rear. There is an ascent of over 500 ft from Abbotsbury onto the hills above the village, which brings its rewards in the shape of far-ranging views across Chesil Beach and the English Channel.

Where to park
In the Rodden Row public car park in the centre of Abbotsbury (GR 578853). **OS map**: Explorer OL15 Purbeck & South Dorset.

How to get there
Abbotsbury lies on the B3157 coast road running between Bridport and Weymouth. The car park is clearly signed and lies at the end of a cul de sac just east of Church Street. Postcode DT3 4JL.

Dog factors
Distance: 5 miles (8 km).
Road walking: A short section of road walking in Abbotsbury. The B3157 has to be crossed on the way to Chesil Beach from the downland.
Livestock: Occasionally livestock will be found in one or two fields on the downland.
Stiles: Three stiles with dog flaps.
Nearest vets: Castle Veterinary Clinic, 624 Dorchester Road, Weymouth DT3 5LH. www.castlevets.co.uk ☎ 01305 813303.

Dorset – A Dog Walker's Guide

Nearest refreshments

Well-behaved dogs on leads are welcome at the Ilchester Arms in Abbotsbury where food is served between 12 noon and 3 pm and 6 pm and 9 pm on weekdays, 12 noon until 9.30 pm on Saturdays and 12 noon until 6 pm on Sundays. www.theilchester.co.uk ☎ 01305 873841. Postcode DT3 4JR.

The Walk

1 Leave the car park and with your dog on a lead, walk up to the B3157. Follow **Rosemary Lane** opposite before turning left into Back Street. After 100 yards, just past Spring Cottage, turn right onto a bridleway signposted to Hardy's Monument and Blind Lane Hillfort. Follow this track uphill for ½ mile to a gate. Continue walking uphill to a junction at which you keep walking towards the hilltop. Beyond another gate, keep ahead to another gate and a rocky outcrop before continuing ahead uphill past an old quarry to a pair of gates on the hilltop. Pass through the left-hand gate and follow the **South Dorset Ridgeway** across the hilltop for one mile, eventually passing a beacon before joining a road where you may need to put a lead on your dog. Cross the road and follow a path opposite and slightly to the left, uphill to reach **Abbotsbury Castle**.

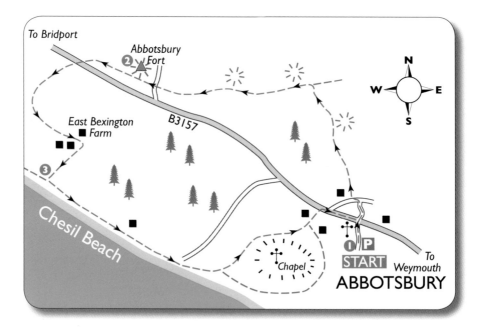

Abbotsbury Fort.

2 Beyond a trig point by the fort, continue following the South Dorset Ridgeway across the hilltop for ½ mile to a stile and the B3157. With your dog on a lead, cross the road, pass through a gate opposite and enter the National Trust **Tulks Hill** property. Walk along to a point where a wall forms a corner and turn left on a path signed to Chesil Beach. Continue down to a stile before walking down the left edge of the next field, with a detached property on the right. At the bottom of the field, follow a path that winds its way round to the next stile before crossing a field diagonally towards **East Bexington Farm** where you may need to put your dog on a lead. Beyond a gate, follow

the path ahead and around the back of the farm to reach a gate and a path that drops down the right edge of a field to reach the **Coast Path** and **Chesil Beach**.

❸ Follow a coastal road at the back of Chesil Beach to the left along to a car park in one mile. Do not enter the car park. Instead veer right onto the beach and follow a rough path across the pebbles of Chesil Beach for 200 yards to a more well-defined path signposted to Abbotsbury. Ignoring all side turns, including one signposted to 'Abbotsbury Village' on the left, continue for 1 ¼ miles to a junction below **Chapel Hill**. Turn left and, with your dog on a lead, walk up to the B3157 before turning right, back to the church and car park.

The Hardy Monument

The Hardy Monument.

In 1896, Thomas Hardy composed a poem entitled *Wessex Heights*. He wrote of Dorset's high places 'shaped as if by a kindly hand'. These were special places 'for thinking, dreaming and dying on'. Hardy would no doubt include Bronkham Hill, the highpoint on this walk, as one such place. Here we have a rolling landscape with views across to the English Channel, a landscape still dominated by grassland rather than arable crops and where little has changed in over 100 years. Overlooking this corner of Dorset is the Hardy Monument, only this time it is dedicated to a different Thomas Hardy, Vice Admiral Sir Thomas Hardy who was a commander at the Battle of Trafalgar. The site was chosen so that the monument was visible from the sea and could be used as a landmark for shipping. From the top of the monument, shaped like a spyglass and with its eight corners aligned with the compass points, it is possible to see Start Point in Devon and St Catherine's Point on the Isle of Wight, as well as Pen Hill in the Mendip Hills. This is a perfect dog walk, with open fields and enclosed tracks that cross a landscape so evocative of Hardy's Wessex.

Dog factors

Distance: 4½ miles (7.2 km).
Road walking: 350 yards of walking on a quiet lane before the climb onto Bronkham Hill.
Livestock: Occasionally sheep will be found grazing in the fields early on in the walk.
Stiles: None.
Nearest vets: Castle Veterinary Clinic, Poundbury Business Centre, Poundbury, Dorchester DT1 3WA. www.castlevets.co.uk
☎ 01305 267083.

Terrain
Well-defined tracks and easy-to-follow field paths; one easy ascent onto Bronkham Hill.

Where to park
Blackdown car park, 200 yards east of the National Trust car park by the Hardy Monument (GR 616877). **OS map**: Explorer OL15 Purbeck & South Dorset.

How to get there
An unclassified road runs between the A35 at Winterbourne Abbas and the

B3157 at Portesham. At a crossroads three miles south of Winterbourne Abbas, follow the side turn signposted to the Hardy Monument. In one mile, drive past the monument and drop downhill for 200 yards to a cattle grid and a parking area on the left at the entrance to the Blackdown Reserve. Postcode DT2 9HY.

Nearest refreshments

Drive back up to the Hardy Monument to find the China Mermaid Retro Café located in a 1970s caravan. This café, with outside seating, is open from Wednesdays to Sundays from Good Friday through to September, weather permitting. www.chinamermaid.com ☎ 01305 871903.

The Walk

. . . .

1 Near the parking area is the entrance to a property called Blackdown. Across the road from this entrance is a footpath signed as the **Jubilee Way**. Ignoring an early right turn to Corton Hill, follow the enclosed path ahead, still the

Waiting patiently to walk.

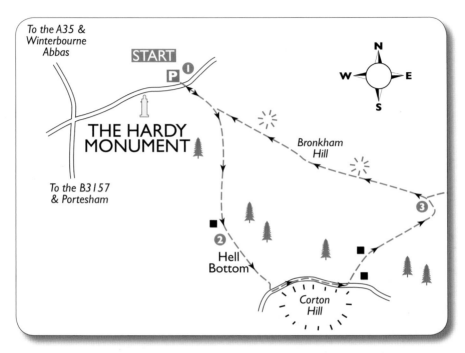

Jubilee Way, for ¼ mile to a gate on the right and the Jubilee Way signposted once again to Corton Hill. Pass through this gateway and walk diagonally across the field to a gap in the hedge at the field boundary. Drop downhill in the following field to a gate before following a grassy track to some farm buildings where you may need to put your dog on a lead.

2 Follow the path ahead across four fields through a valley known as **Hell Bottom**. Early on in the fourth field, pass through a gate on the left and follow an enclosed track to the right along to a junction before turning right, down a section of track to a quiet lane. Follow this lane to the left for 350 yards before turning left along a bridleway that passes two properties before reaching a junction of paths on the hilltop in ¾ mile.

3 Turn left signed to the Hardy Monument, and follow an enclosed path along to a gate and open field. Look out for shake holes and tumuli as you cross this field, before continuing along a section of the **South Dorset Ridgeway** for 1½ miles across Bronkham Hill and back to the car park.

Hardy's Cottage and Puddletown Forest

Hardy's Cottage.

A **delightful walk into the heart of Hardy country.** This is the landscape of Hardy's youth, where he gained inspiration for such fine novels as *Under the Greenwood Tree* and *Far From the Madding Crowd.* Tucked away on the edge of Thorncombe Wood is the charming thatched cottage where Hardy was born in 1840. The cottage was built in 1800 by his great-grandfather, and remained the family home for several generations.

Hardy's grandfather was involved in a small way with brandy smuggling, and added a narrow opening in the porch to look out for excise men! Hardy was much taken with the woodland around the family home, woodland that forms the focus of this walk. Oak, silver birch, larch and chestnut trees provide fine cover for jays, treecreepers, nuthatches and woodpeckers. Mammals, including squirrels, foxes, deer and badgers also make their homes in Thorncombe Wood, where the speckled wood butterfly is a summer resident too. All dogs enjoy the sounds and smells in woodland, and this walk will provide just that.

Terrain
Well-defined tracks and paths through an undulating area of woodland.

Where to park
Hardy's Cottage car park (GR 725922 or postcode DT2 8QJ). **OS map**: Explorer OL15 Purbeck & South Dorset.

How to get there
As the A35 approaches Dorchester from the north-east, there is a roundabout at its junction with the B3150. Leave this roundabout to follow the unclassified road to Higher Bockhampton. At a crossroads after one mile, take the left turn signed to Hardy's Cottage. In ½ mile, follow the right turn signposted to the car park and National Trust visitor centre. Postcode DT2 8QJ.

Nearest refreshments
There is a café at the visitor centre at Hardy's Cottage. It is an independent family business that uses local produce where possible and offers everything from homemade cakes and scones to freshly prepared soups and sandwiches. Dogs are very welcome at the café where the owner is a great dog lover, known to give out free gravy bones and other dog treats. The visitor centre is open every day from 10 am until 4 pm.

Dog factors
· ·
Distance: 4 miles (6.4 km).
Road walking: None.
Livestock: None.
Stiles: None.
Nearest vets: Southfield Veterinary Centre, South Walks, Dorchester, DT1 1TU. www.southfieldvet.co.uk. ☎ 01305 262913.

The Walk

1 As you enter the car park, there is an information board on the left. Follow the woodland path alongside this board signposted to Hardy's Cottage. Follow the path through to **Hardy's Cottage**, ignoring the path on the left into its garden, instead keeping on the main path that runs behind the property to reach a monument to Thomas Hardy. Turn right and follow a path beyond a metal barrier into **Puddletown Forest**. In 200 yards, keep ahead at a crossroads. In another 100 yards at a major junction of paths, keep ahead on a bridleway.

2 After 600 yards, at a junction, two paths go off to the right. Take the first of these paths that drops downhill to reach a broad track. Follow the path opposite into the heart of the woodland. In 200 yards at a T-junction, follow a bridleway to the right and, at a crossroads in ½ mile, turn right. Follow the path ahead for 600 yards to a point where it climbs uphill to reach a T-junction. Turn left and follow a path across open heathland before dropping downhill and onto a crossroads in ½ mile.

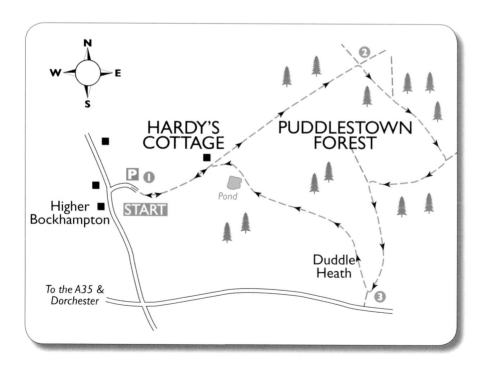

3 Turn right and follow a path beyond a wooden barrier through an area of rhododendrons and coniferous trees to a gate and the open **Duddle Heath** in ¼ mile. Walk across this heathland and uphill to a crossroads of paths. Follow the path opposite, signposted to Hardy's Cottage, passing a pond on the left. In 400 yards, the path reaches a junction at the rear of the cottage. Turn left and follow the path to the visitor centre. From the visitor centre, turn left back to the car park.

RG taking a break.

Portland Bill

Portland Bill.

The Isle of Portland is in fact a peninsula, linked to the mainland by an 18-mile strip of shingle known as Chesil Beach. Portland Bill is the southern tip of this peninsula and is the site of rugged limestone cliffs, a pair of lighthouses and a number of small caves. Portland Bill was a notorious ships' graveyard so it came as no surprise when George I issued a patent for a lighthouse to be constructed here in 1716. Originally the light was based upon enclosed lanterns and coal fires, a far cry from today's light with its intensity of 674,000 candela and a range of 25 nautical miles. The landscape around Portland Bill is dotted with quarries and workings dating back to the Middle Ages. Extensive quarrying started in the 17th century, with the industry peaking in 1899 with 1,441 workers. Portland stone has a global reputation, having been used in such illustrious buildings as St Paul's Cathedral and the United Nations building in New York. This is a wild and exciting coastal walk, with fine sea views and a rich array of seabirds.

Dog factors

Distance: 3½ miles (5.6 km).
Road walking: There is a short section of road walking near Southwell but there is a pavement.
Livestock: None.
Stiles: None.
Nearest vets: Moorcroft Veterinary Practice, 38 Easton Street, Easton, Portland, DT5 1BT. www.medivet.co.uk ☎ 01305 823301.

Terrain
Generally level coastal paths; the walk from East Cliff back to Portland Bill is stony and uneven in places.

Where to park
Portland Bill car park (GR 677685 or postcode DT5 2JT). **OS map**: Explorer OL15 Purbeck & South Dorset.

How to get there
Follow the A354 southwards from Weymouth to Easton, in the centre of Portland. Beyond Easton, a signposted road leads to Portland Bill where the car park is clearly signed. Postcode DT5 2JT.

Nearest refreshments
The Lobster Pot by the car park, one of the top 25 most charming seaside cafés according to the *Daily Telegraph*, has an outside patio area where dogs are welcome. The Lobster Pot is open seven days a week. www.lobsterpotrestaurantportland.co.uk ☎ 01305 820242. Postcode DT5 2JT.

The Walk

1 Walk to the top end of the car park, walking away from the lighthouse. Follow a path that crosses the entrance to an MoD base on the left and continue

across open grassland to reach the coast. Turn right and walk uphill towards a coastguard's lookout station.

2 Walk 350 yards beyond the lookout station then follow a path on the right signposted to **East Cliff**, one field before another MoD base. When this path

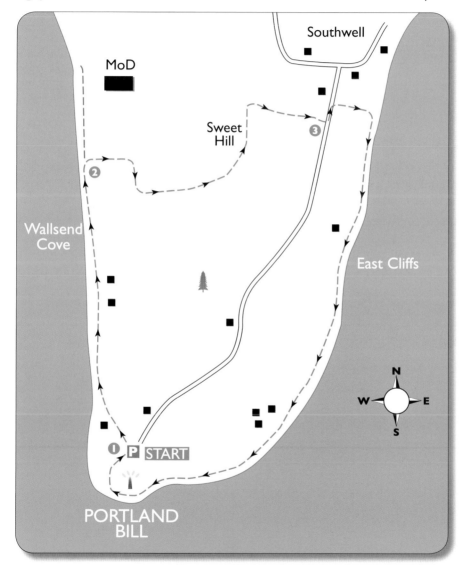

reaches the corner of the field ahead, turn right and, in 100 yards, bear left to reach a junction after 25 yards. Ignoring the path going off to the right, follow the path ahead to a junction in 150 yards. Turn left to follow a path that runs between drystone walls. In ¼ mile, just past some stables, pass through a handgate on the right and follow an enclosed path down to the road that runs from Southwell to Portland Bill, ignoring one right turn along the way.

3 With your dog on a lead, follow a pavement to the left for 150 yards and, by a 30 mph sign, follow a path on the right down to the coast. Turn right and follow the **Coast Path** for just over one mile back to **Portland Bill**. There are several paths that all head in the same direction; the most spectacular is the one that clings to the coast. Just before Portland Bill, pass through a collection of beach huts, continue past the lighthouse to reach the Pulpit Rock and turn right to return to the car park.

Beach huts in Portland.

Ringstead Bay

The Coast Path.

Ringstead Bay would be the sort of place that would be the ideal backdrop for filming 'Five Go Down to the Sea'. There are cliffs and a beach, woodland and hay meadows, as well as rather fine holiday homes where Aunt Fanny and Uncle Quentin might well have taken a summer holiday. An element of mystery is provided by the secluded White Nothe Cottages, former coastguard properties, as well as a Second World War bunker that was part of the RAF's radar defence set-up. Then there is St Catherine's church, looking more like a large garden shed, with a modern stained-glass window by Simon Whistler, son of Laurence. This is a fine walk, where tracks cross open countryside before reaching the Coast Path. The views throughout are far-ranging, stretching from the nearby Undercliff out as far as Portland.

Terrain
Well-defined tracks and an easy-to-follow coast path; one steep climb at the end of the walk back to the car park.

Where to park
The National Trust's Ringstead Bay car park (GR 757825). **OS map**: Explorer OL15 Purbeck & South Dorset.

How to get there
Leave the A353 one mile east of Osmington to follow an unclassified road signposted to 'Ringstead Bay and Tearooms'. Having passed through the village of Upton, continue along this lane for one mile, ignoring a right turn to the tearooms, to reach the NT Ringstead Bay car park. Park as close to the entrance as possible, just past a pair of information boards on the right. Postcode DT2 8NQ.

Nearest refreshments
The open grassland alongside the car park is a perfect spot for a picnic, but if you don't fancy that the Ringstead Bay Tearooms is worth a visit.

Dog factors
. . . .

Distance: 4½ miles (7.2 km).
Road walking: None.
Livestock: In the field between the Coast Path and South Down Farm.
Stiles: One, but it is dog-friendly.
Nearest vets: Castle Veterinary Clinic, 624 Dorchester Road, Weymouth, DT3 5LH. www.castlevets.co.uk ☎ 01305 813303.

The Walk
. . . .

1 Walk to the eastern end of the car park, pass through a gate and follow the

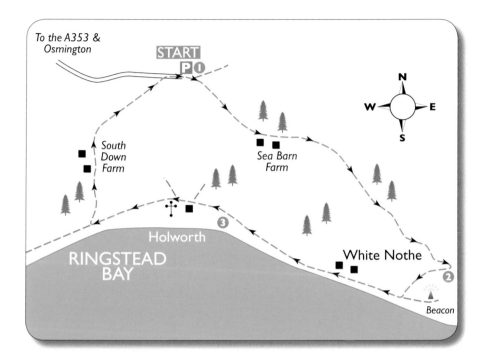

track ahead. In ¼ mile, on a right-hand bend, pass through a handgate ahead and continue following the track towards a stone barn. Having passed the barn, continue along the track for 600 yards to a point where it climbs to reach the top corner of a field. Continue along the path as it bears right and, in 40 yards, turn left through a gateway on a path signed to Daggers Gate and West Lulworth.

2 In ½ mile, just past a chalk pit on the left, pass through a gateway and turn sharply right to follow the line of a fence down to a gate in the bottom corner of the field and the Coast Path. Turn right and follow the path signposted to Ringstead and White Nothe. In 600 yards, having passed **White Nothe Cottages**, continue following the Coast Path above the undercliff along to a gate. Drop downhill on a wide grassy path towards some woodland.

3 At the bottom of the hill, pass through a gate to reach a junction. Continue ahead towards Ringstead, passing through a copse and ignoring the path on the right signposted as the 'Coast Path to Ringstead Bay'. At a junction just past the rear of **Holworth Cottage**, continue ahead along a tarmac lane to reach a small church. Continue along the Coast Path for 350 yards, cross two footbridges and, in 100 yards, cross a stile on the right to follow a path signposted to **NT South Down**. Cross a field to a gate opposite before following a track uphill, passing **South Down Farm**, to return to the car park.

A popular dog walk.

Tolpuddle

Woodland near Tolpuddle.

Tolpuddle **is an attractive village,** lying alongside the somewhat infamous river Piddle. The manor and the 13th-century stone and flint church will catch the eye of the historian, as will the inevitable connections with those Tolpuddle Martyrs. It was here during the first half of the 19th century that 'six men of Dorset' used to meet and discuss how the lot of the local agricultural workers could be improved. Eventually, for the part that each played in 'the administration of an illegal oath', this small group of pioneering trade unionists were sentenced to transportation to Australia. From the old sycamore where the martyrs allegedly met, this walk heads south to explore Southover Heath. Woodland paths bordered with foxgloves and rhododendron bushes dominate this delightful section of the walk, where the strange depressions in the ground are a series of shake holes. Dogs will quite simply enjoy running free through woodland where it is likely that James Hammett, the only martyr to return to the village of his youth, no doubt walked in the first half of the 19th century.

Dog factors

Distance: 6 miles (9.6 km).
Road walking: A short section of quiet lane in Tolpuddle.
Livestock: Possibly in one field near Admiston Farm.
Stiles: None.
Nearest vets: Piddle Valley Vets, The Surgery, Backwater, Puddletown DT2 8SD. www.piddlevalleyvets.co.uk. ☎ 01305 848820.

Terrain
Well-defined field paths and tracks.

Where to park
At a junction in the centre of Tolpuddle by the Martyrs Memorial Shelter, where a lane is signposted to Southover and Affpuddle (GR792945). **OS map**: Explorer 117 Cerne Abbas & Bere Regis.

How to get there
Leave the A35 at its junction with the A354 at Puddletown, 5 miles north-east of Dorchester. Drive into Puddletown, turning left in the village on an unclassified road signposted to Tolpuddle. Postcode DT2 7ES.

Nearest refreshments
The Martyrs Inn in Tolpuddle welcomes everybody including children, dogs and muddy boots. The pub is open from 11 am until 11 pm every day, with food being served from 12 noon to 9 pm. www.themartyrsinn.co.uk. ☎ 01305 848249. Postcode DT2 7ES.

The Walk

1 Follow the lane signposted to Southover and Affpuddle for 350 yards to a point where it bears left by 'The Lodge'. Immediately past this property, turn right onto a track signposted to **Southover Farm**. In 75 yards, where the main track bears right to the farm, keep ahead along a track than runs past a thatched cottage. In ½ mile at a junction, turn left and follow a track around the perimeter of a field to the first of two gateways on the far side of the field. Pass through the first gateway and walk across the left edge of a field towards some coniferous woodland. Enter the woodland in the corner of the field and turn right on a path that initially borders the edge of the woodland.

2 Ignoring all side turns, follow the main path ahead for ¾ mile to a metal barrier and a broad forestry road. Follow this track to the right through the woodland for 1¼ miles to a gate on the left and an open field. Turn right and walk down the right edge of the field to a gate in its next corner and re-enter woodland. An obvious path goes off on the right – ignore this path and follow the narrow path ahead that borders the edge of the woodland to reach a gate on the left. Turn right and walk down to a gate in the corner of the field ahead, a thatched cottage on the right. Follow the track ahead down to a concrete road by **Admiston Farm**.

3 Turn right and, in 20 yards, pass through a gate on the right into a field and walk ahead into the 'main body' of the field before walking diagonally across

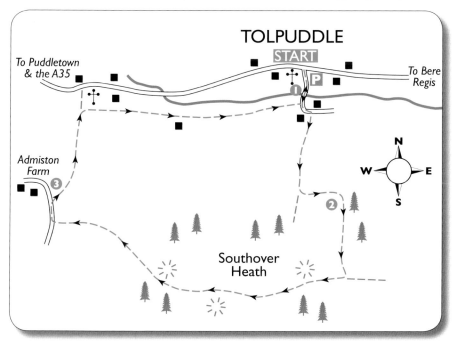

the middle of the field to a gate and **Cowpound Wood**. Follow the path ahead through the woods and on downhill to reach Athelhampton church in ¼ mile. Turn right just before the church and follow a green lane along to **Park Cottage** before following a path along the side of an arable field and on to a gate and **Park Farm**. Follow the road away from Park Farm for ½ mile to a property on the right. Just before this property, pass through a gate on the left and walk across a paddock and along a grassy path to reach a gate and the lane followed at the outset. Retrace your steps to the left along this lane back into Tolpuddle.

The Martyrs' Shelter.

Wareham Forest

Conifers on the heath.

A **heath is a very special habitat.** Heaths only grow in a few areas around Britain – including Dorset – but these precious landscapes are fast disappearing. Similar heaths can be found in Europe but worldwide they are very rare – in fact they are now rarer than tropical rain forests! Dorset's heathlands once covered over 50,000 hectares, stretching from the Avon valley in the east to Dorchester in the west. Changes in agricultural practice, conifer planting, scrub encroachment, urban expansion and road building have all contributed to a reduction in area to about 7,000 hectares today. These Dorset heaths boast all six species of reptiles found in the United

Dorset – A Dog Walker's Guide

Kingdom – adders, grass snakes, common lizards, slow worms, smooth snakes and sand lizards. All of this will no doubt be lost on dogs, who will simply enjoy running free in a landscape with no cars or livestock.

Terrain
Well-defined tracks and paths that cross an open area of heathland.

Where to park
Wareham Forest car park at a point shown as Stroud Bridge on the OS map (GR 889916). **OS map**: Explorer OL15 Purbeck & South Dorset.

How to get there
An unclassified road links the A351 near Wareham station with the A35 east of Bere Regis. From Wareham, it is signposted to Bere Regis. Three miles from Wareham, having passed Wareham Forest Tourist Park, turn right into a gravelled parking area where a bridleway leaves the road. There is no signage and the turning can be easily missed. This parking area should not be confused with the next parking area, 200 yards further along the road. Postcode BH20 7NZ.

Nearest refreshments
The Silent Woman Inn lies 1½ miles south of the car park, on the road back to Wareham. The pub has extensive gardens where dogs are welcome – but note that children are not allowed in the bar areas. Closed on Mondays, the Silent Woman serves food from 12 noon to 2 pm and 6 pm to 9 pm, other than Sundays when food is only available at lunchtimes. www.thesilentwoman. co.uk ☎ 01929 552909. Postcode BH20 7PA.

Dog factors
Distance: 4 miles (6.4 km).
Road walking: None.
Livestock: None.
Stiles: None.
Nearest vets: Wareham Veterinary Centre, 17 East Street, Wareham, BH20 4NN. www.thepethealthpartnership.co.uk ☎ 01929 552599.

The Walk

1 Beyond a metal barrier at the end of the parking area, follow a forestry road

for ¼ mile to a junction with a pylon visible ahead. Turn right to a crossroads in ¼ mile, continue to another junction in 200 yards and keep following the main track ahead signposted as the Sika Cycle Trail. At a T-junction in ½ mile, by a seat, turn left. At a crossroads in ½ mile, keep ahead, pass under some electricity cables and continue for 250 yards to the next crossroads.

2 Keep ahead and, in ¼ mile, where the open heathland ends and coniferous woodland begins, turn left along a gravelled forestry road. In ¼ mile, beyond a gate, turn left at a T-junction with Woolsbarrow hillfort to the right. In 175 yards, veer right, off the main path, to follow a path up the eastern flank of

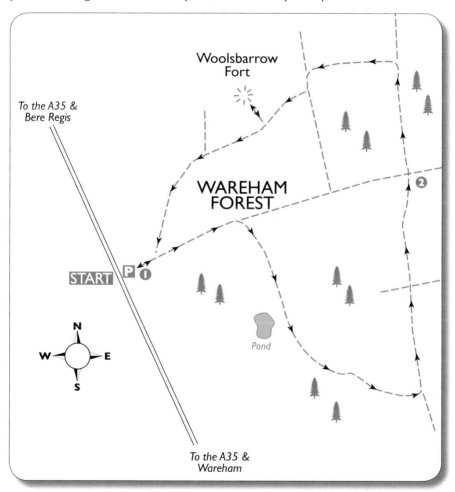

Dorset – A Dog Walker's Guide

the hillfort. At a junction in 200 yards by a hillfort sign, detour to the right to explore the heart of the hillfort. For the main walk, turn left and drop downhill to a junction by another hillfort sign. Follow the path to the right for 500 yards to a junction where two paths go off to the right. Take the first path that returns the walk to the car park.

Heathland track.

Corfe Castle

A magnificent ruin

Corfe Castle fully deserves that much used adjective 'iconic'. Seated atop a steep hill in a gap in a long line of chalk hills, the castle dates back to the 11th century and the time of William the Conqueror. It was twice besieged by Parliamentarian forces during the Civil War. The first siege in 1643 was unsuccessful but by 1645, being one of the last remaining Royalist strongholds in the south, siege and assault became inevitable, leaving today's magical ruin. The Corfe Castle area resounds with nostalgia, and not just because of the castle. The Swanage Railway runs through the village, bringing with it the sights and sounds of the bygone era of steam. The station in Corfe Castle dates from the late 19th century, narrowly escaping demolition in the 1970s. Its signal box and waiting rooms, freight shed and station master's lounge, have grown men reliving the memories of their long-gone youth. The walk explores the chalk hills to the east of Corfe Castle, where the Purbeck Way running across the hilltop is perfect dog-walking country. Dogs can run free on this unimproved chalk grassland, whilst their owners will enjoy the far ranging views across the Isle of Purbeck, and wallow in nostalgia as steam trains make their way from Norden through to Swanage.

Terrain
The footpath below the chalk hills can be overgrown in places during summer months. One climb followed by easy hilltop walking.

Where to park
The Challow Walkers' car park (GR 964822). **OS map**: Explorer OL15 Purbeck & South Dorset.

How to get there
Drive into Corfe Castle from Wareham and, on a right-hand bend below the castle and with Brook Cottage ahead, turn left into Sandy Hill Lane. Pass under a railway bridge and in 200 yards turn left into the Challow Walkers' car park opposite a right turn to Challow Farm. Postcode BH20 5JF.

Nearest refreshments
Unsurprisingly, the Greyhound Inn in Corfe Castle is a dog-friendly pub. Fresh food is served all day throughout the year. www.greyhoundcorfe.co.uk ☎ 01929 480205. Postcode BH20 5EZ.

Dog factors
. . . .
Distance: 3 miles (4.8 km).
Road walking: None.
Livestock: Very occasionally on the hilltops.
Stiles: None.
Nearest vets: Lynwood Vets, 87 Ulwell Road, Swanage, BH19 1QU. www.lynwoodvets.co.uk ☎ 01929 422213.

That's my stick!

The Walk

1 With your dog on a lead for the first few minutes of the walk, leave the car park, back out to **Sandy Hill Lane** and turn left. After a few paces, bear left on a footpath signposted as the **Purbeck Way**. Beyond a gateway, follow the path ahead as it runs below a hillside on the left. In 200 yards, at a junction with a marker stone, bear right on the **Underhill Path** to Ulwell. In ½ mile, at a gateway with an aerial mast on the hilltop to the left, keep ahead across more open countryside, the path having been in bushes to this point. Shortly a track crosses the path. Ignoring this track, continue for ¾ mile to a junction with a broad chalky track.

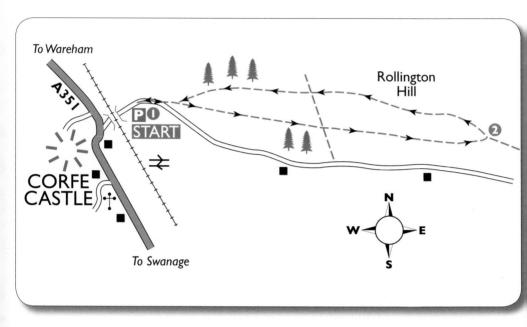

2 Turn sharply left to walk up to a marker post on the hilltop. Follow the path to the left back towards Corfe Castle. Beyond a gate, continue walking across the hilltop towards the aerial mast. Pass through a gate and, at a marker stone, take the path to the left that drops downhill to rejoin a section of path followed at the outset. Follow this path back towards **Sandy Hill Lane**. As you approach the road put your dog on a lead. Turn right along the road and walk back to the car park. *NOTE: For a much longer walk, continue along the Underhill Path for another 1½ miles before turning sharply left up onto Nine Barrow Down and following the hilltop path – the Purbeck Way – back towards Corfe Castle.*

Studland and Old Harry

Old Harry Rocks.

Studland offers visitors one of Britain's cleanest beaches, with excellent views that stretch across Poole Harbour to Bournemouth and beyond. The village church dedicated to St Nicholas is very much a Norman construction, a sturdy stone building with chancel, nave and low saddleback tower. The corbel table that runs the length of the nave, adorned with grotesque carved faces, will certainly prove amusing! The village is the starting point for this excellent walk that climbs up onto the open expanses of Ballard Down, a chalk headland that looks across to the Needles and the Isle of Wight. At the furthest extremity of the headland stand a number of impressive chalk stacks, the most notable of which has earned the title of Old Harry. These fine natural features have become a popular nesting spot with cormorants and other sea birds. Dogs will enjoy running free on the open expanses of Ballard Down, although livelier animals may need their leads on when walking the clifftop path above the chalk stacks.

Terrain
Well-defined field paths and tracks; one climb onto Ballard Down.

Where to park
The National Trust car park in Studland by the Bankes Arms (GR 037826 or postcode BH19 3AU). **OS map**: Explorer OL15 Purbeck & South Dorset.

How to get there
Follow the B3351 from Corfe Castle through to Studland. Immediately before the Studland Stores, take the turning on the right signed to the church. In ¼ mile, this road bears sharply left and passes in front of the Bankes Arms. The National Trust car park is next to the pub. Postcode BH19 3AU.

Nearest refreshments
The Bankes Arms in Studland welcomes well-behaved dogs and their owners. Open all year round, other than Christmas Day, food is served from 12 noon until 9.30 pm between June and October, and at lunchtimes and in the evenings during the off-peak season. www.bankesarms.com ☎ 01929 450225. Postcode BH19 3AU.

Dog factors
Distance: 4 miles (6.4 km).
Road walking: A small section in Studland, and approaching Ballard Down as far as the Glebeland Estate.
Livestock: Very occasionally on Ballard Down.
Stiles: None.
Nearest vets: AfriVet Veterinary Clinic, 25 Woodside Road, Parkstone, Poole, BH14 9JH. www.afrivet.com. ☎ 01202 722739.

The Walk

❶ Leave the car park, turn left and shortly turn left along a footpath signed to 'The Church'. Walk through the churchyard and down **Church Road** to a junction. Drop down to Manor Farm and follow the cul de sac around to the right that runs past the farm's tea rooms and on towards Ballard Down. Follow this road ahead for ½ mile as it climbs uphill to reach a small housing development called **Glebeland Estate**.

❷ Immediately past the last property – Summer Hill – where the road bears right, pass through a gate on the left-hand side and follow a track uphill onto **Ballard Down**. In 350 yards, by a bench on the hilltop, follow the path to the left, signposted to 'Old Harry', for ¾ mile to a trig point.

❸ Drop downhill to a gate in ¼ mile before following the **Coast Path** along the eastern end of the headland. There are steep chalk cliffs below on the right so be sure to have your dog under control. In ¾ mile, having reached Old Harry and the end of the headland, turn left and walk across the open grassland to reach a path running into some bushes. Follow this path for one mile, back

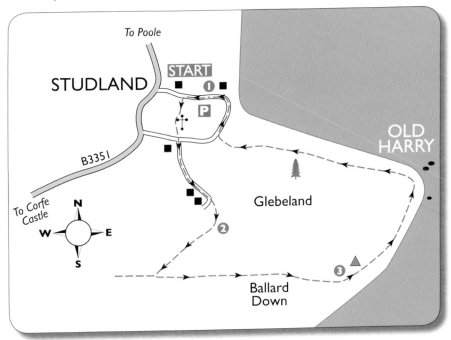

to the road in Studland and some public conveniences. Turn right back to the Bankes Arms and the NT car park.

View towards Poole.

St Aldhelm's Head

View of Winspit.

This walk explores one of the more dramatically rugged stretches of coastline in Dorset. St Aldhelm's Head, 350 ft above the English Channel, is dominated by a Norman Chapel whose turreted roof once supported a brazier. Its job was to warn sailors of the treacherous rocks at the foot of the cliffs. One vessel that did come to grief here was the East Indiaman *Halsewell*. She was wrecked in 1786, with 168 members of her 250 strong crew being drowned. Before St Aldhelm's Head is Winspit Bottom, where the cliffs were the site of extensive quarrying. Here there is a network of easy-to-explore passages and tunnels where villagers from Worth Matravers, a delightful stone village that lies at the start of the walk, found many of the bodies washed ashore from the *Halsewell*. Incidentally, if you and your dog are walking this way at dawn on Easter Sunday, you will be able to celebrate Holy Communion in St Aldhelm's Chapel at one of the most picturesque settings in England ... but put any restless pooch onto a lead because it is a long drop down to the sea!

Terrain

Well-defined tracks and field paths lead to the coast; the Coast Path is clearly signed.

Where to park

The public car park in Worth Matravers (GR 974777). **OS map**: Explorer OL15 Purbeck & South Dorset.

How to get there

Leave the A351 at Corfe Castle to follow the B3069 to Kingston. One mile on from Kingston, leave this 'B' road and follow an unclassified road into Worth Matravers. The car park is on the right as you enter the village. Postcode BH19 3LE.

Nearest refreshments

The Square & Compass in Worth Matravers has been in the hands of the Newman Family for over 100 years. It remains unchanging and unspoilt and, as befits such a traditional pub, is dog-friendly. Open lunchtimes and evenings on winter weekdays, and all day at weekends. Open all day during summer months. www.squareandcompasspub.co.uk ☎ 01929 439229. Postcode BH19 3LF.

Dog factors

Distance: 4 miles (6.4 km).
Road walking: Short sections of quiet lane in Worth Matravers.
Livestock: Occasionally in a field en route to the coast.
Stiles: None.
Nearest vets: Lynwood Vets, 87 Ulwell Road, Swanage, BH19 1QU. www.lynwoodvets.co.uk ☎ 01929 422213.

St Aldhelm's Chapel.

The Walk

. . . .

1 Leave the car park, turn right and walk down to a junction by the Square & Compass. Turn right and follow a cul de sac to a green. Follow the road along the left edge of the green to reach a rank of properties called **London Row**. Turn left down the lane in front of these properties heading to Winspit. Beyond the last property, follow an enclosed footpath down to a gate before walking the length of a field to a gate at its end, all the while walking towards the sea. Beyond this gate, follow a path for 200 yards to a track and continue along this track for 600 yards down to **Winspit**.

2 Just before reaching the coast, follow the **Coast Path** to the right up some steps signposted to St Aldhelm's Head. It is worth detouring ahead to the

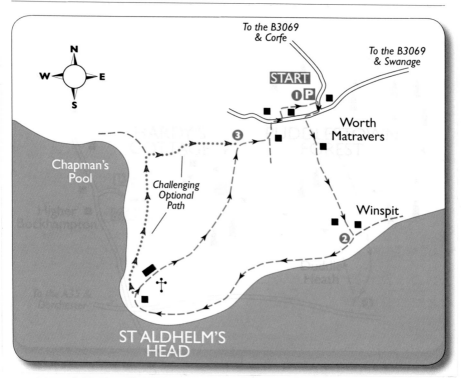

sea to explore the disused quarries on the coast. Follow the path to the Coastguard Station at St Aldhelm's Head. Follow a track to the right past St Aldhelm's chapel and a rank of cottages to reach a car park on the left in just under 1½ miles.

3 At this point, pass through a gateway on the right and follow a path across a field and along a section of farm track to a lane by **Weston Farm**. Turn left up to a road junction, where a dog lead may be necessary, before turning right towards Worth Matravers. In 350 yards, follow a footpath on the left up through a recreation ground to a stile in the top corner. Continue along the footpath ahead and, having passed through two gateways, enter an open field. Turn right and walk across three small fields before following a footpath down to the road by the Square & Compass. Turn left back to the car park. *NOTE: From the Coastguard Station at St Aldhelm's Head, it is possible to continue along the Coast Path for 1 mile to a point above Chapman's Pool before heading inland to the car park mentioned in Point 2. This is a spectacular path but does involve a huge descent and ascent using flights of steps that dogs – and their owners – might find difficult.*

APPENDIX

The following vets are located close to the walks:

AfriVet Veterinary Clinic
25 Woodside Road, Parkstone, Poole, BH14 9JH.
www.afrivet.com. ☎ 01202 722739.

Bredy Veterinary Centre
Sea Road North, Bridport, DT6 4RR.
www.bredyvets.co.uk. ☎ 01308 456771.

Castle Veterinary Clinic
Poundbury Business Centre, Poundbury, Dorchester DT1 3WA.
www.castlevets.co.uk ☎ 01305 267083.

Castle Veterinary Clinic
624 Dorchester Road, Weymouth DT3 5LH.
www.castlevets.co.uk. ☎ 01305 813303.

Damory Veterinary Clinic
Edward Street, Blandford Forum, DT11 7QT.
www.damoryvets.co.uk ☎ 01258 452626.

Friars Moor Vets
Higher Shaftesbury Road, Blandford Forum, DT11 8ST.
www.friarsmoorvets.co.uk ☎ 01258 472160.

Girling and Bowditch Veterinary Surgeons
Bull Lane, Maiden Newton, DT2 0BQ.
www.beaminstervets.co.uk. ☎ 01308 862312.

Girling and Bowditch Veterinary Surgeons
Beaminster, DT8 3HB.
www.beaminstervets.co.uk. ☎ 01308 862312.

Longmead Veterinary Practice
Little Content Lane, Shaftesbury, SP7 8PL.
www.longmeadvets.co.uk ☎ 01747 852064.

Lynwood Vets
87 Ulwell Road, Swanage, BH19 1QU.
www.lynwoodvets.co.uk. ☎ 01929 422213.

Moorcroft Veterinary Practice
38 Easton Street, Easton, Portland, DT5 1BT.
www.medivet.co.uk. ☎ 01305 823301.

Piddle Valley Vets
The Surgery, Backwater, Puddletown DT2 8SD.

OTHER TITLES FROM COUNTRYSIDE BOOKS

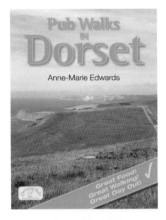
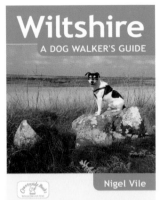
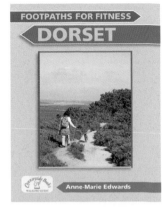

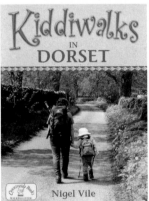
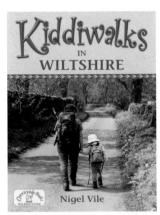
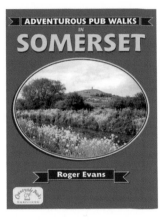

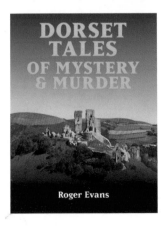
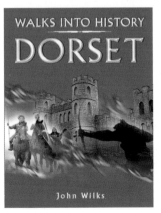

To see the full range of books by Countryside Books then visit
www.countrysidebooks.co.uk

Follow us on